Growing Up **Black,**
Angry and In **Love**

The Story of a Young Man

Anthony Williams

authorHOUSE®

AuthorHouse™
1663 Liberty Drive
Bloomington, IN 47403
www.authorhouse.com
Phone: 1-800-839-8640

First published by AuthorHouse 5/11/2009

ISBN: 978-1-4389-6593-2 (sc)

Printed in the United States of America
Bloomington, Indiana

This book is printed on acid-free paper.

FROM: Anthony Williams (anthony.williams73@yahoo.com)
TO: antohny.williams73@yahoo.com
DATE: Sunday, July 13, 2008 2:24:32 PM
SUBJECT:

(GROWING UP YOUNG,BLACK,ANGRY AND IN LOVE)

THE STORY OF A YOUNG MAN

BY; ANTHONY WILLIAMS

FROM: ANTHONY WILLIAMS (ANTHONY.WILLIAMS73@YAHOO.COM)

TO: ANTOHNY.WILLIAMS73@YAHOO.COM

DATE: THURSDAY 15, 2008 5:54:12 PM

SUBJECT:

(GROWING UP BLACK, ANGRY AND IN LOVE) BY ANTHONY WILLIAMS GROWING UP AT THE AGE OF SEVEN, I STARTED REALIZING THAT PEOPLE WHERE DIFFERENT, I WAS BROWN, SOME PEOPLE WAS DARK AND SOME WHITE. I STARTED FIGURING OUT THAT EVERYONE WAS NOT THE SAME. BUT ONE THING I DID KNOW , WAS I LIKE GIRLS. SO BY AGE 13, I THOUGHT I WAS A PRETTY BOY, BUT I WAS SHY AND SCARY. WE HAD A NIEGHBOR HOOD GIRL WAS ABOUT AGE 17. SHE ALWAYS WANTED TO SEDUCE US. BUT ME, I WAS YOUNG AND DUMB, I ALWAYS RUN AND HIDE. AT THE SAME TIME, I THOUGHT I WAS BAD. I STARTED FIGHTS ON MY BLOCK, WITH THE NIEGHBORHOOD KIDS, I ALWAYS WON. I COULD FIGHT BUT GIRLS WAS MY MAIN CONCERN. I LOVE LADIES, ARE GIRLS, I WOULDN'T SLEEP WITH THEM BECAUSE, I HAD A GOOD MOM AND DAD. PLUS I WAS SCARED OF MY MOTHER , SHE DID NOT PLAY. I HATED THE FACT THAT MY MOM AND DAD WORKED SO HARD TO FEED 8 KIDS. BUT MY PARENTS WOULD ALWAYS MAKE SURE WE HAD SOMETHING TO EAT. WE WERE VERY POOR , THATS WERE THE ANGER CAME IN. MY MOM AND DAD WORKED LIKED DOGS FOR US.WE SOME TIMES HAD TO SHARE CLOTHES AND EVEN WEAR THEM TWICE.

FROM: Anthony Williams (anthony.williams73@yahoo.com)

To: antohny.williams73@yahoo.com

Date: Thursday, May 29, 2008 3:38:40 PM

Subject:

AT AGE 18, I STARTED MY INTERST IN OLDER LADIES. I LIKE THEM BECAUSE THEY ALEADY HAD THINGS IN LIFE. LIKE CARS AND HOUSES. I MEET A FEW LADIES AND ACTUALLY PLAYED THEM. I HAD A LADIE IN EVERY NIEGHBORHOOD. I HAD ONE FOR FOOD ,WHEN I WAS HUNGRY AND ONE FOR MONEY WHEN I NEED IT.THEN I STARTED THINKING , I NEED TO MAKE SOMETHING OUT OF MY SELF. I SAID I WOULD GET A JOB, I TRIED TO GET ONE BUT NO ONE WOULD HIRE ME EVEN MCDONALDS. SO I WENT TO TRADE SCHOOL FOR COOKING. AFTER AWHILE,I BECAME VERY GOOD IN COOKING. EVEN THOUGH I WAS DOING GOOD , I COULDN'T STOP THINKIN ABOUT LADIES. SO ONE DAY MY BROTHER HAD HIS GIRL FRIEND OVER AND SHE BOUGHT A FRIEND. SHE WAS SO BEAUTIFUL TO ME. I DID NOT APPROACH HER,BUT SHE APPROACH ME A COUPLE OF DAYS LATER.I FELL IN LOVE QUICK, SHE LIKE ME AND I LIKE HER. I WAS ALWAYS A VIRGIN UNTIL I MEET HER. EVEN THOUGH,PEOPLE THOUGHT I WAS A LADIES MAN. AFTER HAVING SEX THE FIRST TIME , I WAS ADDICTED TO IT. I WAS A SEX ADDICT.

FROM: ANTHONY WILLIAMS (ANTHONY.WILLIAMS73@YAHOO.COM)

TO: ANTOHNY.WILLIAMS73@YAHOO.COM

DATE: SATURDAY, MAY 31, 2008 4:59:12 PM

SUBJECT:

THE ONLY THING ON MY MIND WAS,SEX AND MONEY.
I FINISH COOKING SCHOOL AT ABOUT AGE 20.
I WENT OUT THIER PUTTING IN APLICATIONS,EVEN THOUGH IT SEEMS LIKE NO ONE WOULD HIRE ME.
I SAID I WENT TO SCHOOL FOR NOTHING.
SO I TOOK A LOOK AT MY LIFE.
AN I WAS WATCHING A TALKSHOW ONE DAY ,A DRUG DEALER WAS ON IT.
HE TALKED ABOUT HOW HE TOOK TWENTY DOLLARS AND BOUGHT DRUGS WITH IT.
THE DRUG DEALER BECAME RICH, SO I SAID I CAN DO THAT.
I GOT TWENTY DOLLARS AND WENT GOT ME SOME DRUGS FROM A FRIEND OF MINDS.
I PUT THE WORD OUT THAT I HAD IT,AND STARTED MAKING MONEY.

FROM: Anthony Williams (anthony.williams73@yahoo.com)

TO: antohny.williams73@yahoo.com

DATE: Saturday, May 31, 2008 5:13:43 PM

SUBJECT:

SINCE I STARTED MAKING MONEY ,LADIES STARTED NOTICING ME.

I HAD POWER AND MONEY,LADIES STARTED SEDUCING ME.

I HAD A WOMAN IN EVERY HOOD, ONE FOR MONEY,ONE FOR FOOD ARE SEX AND SOME WERE TO STAY.

IWAS DOING GOOD, IDID IT FOR ABOUT A YEAR ,THEN I REALIZED ,I WAS GETTING TO POPULAR.

I KNEW EVENTALLY ,I WOULD BE IN JAIL ARE DEAD.

SO I THOUGHT ABOUT MY LIFE AND SAID MY MOTHER RAISED ME BETTER THAN THIS.

SO I TOOK MY DRUG MONEY AND SPENT EVERY DIME LOOKING FOR A JOB.

FROM: ANTHONY WILLIAMS (ANTHONY.WILLIAMS73@YAHOO.COM)

TO: ANTOHNY.WILLIAMS73@YAHOO.COM

DATE: SUNDAY, JUNE 1, 2008 2:24:18 PM

SUBJECT:

IT WAS ROUGH FOR A WHILE,I HAD THESE IN AND OUT JOBS.

THAT WAS NOT GETTING ME ANY WERE,SO I TOOK THE EASY WAY OUT AND STARTED HUSTLING WOMEN AGAIN.

I EVENTUALLY MEET A OLDER LADY WHO WAS ,ABOUT 34 AND AM IN MY EARLY 20'S.

SHE ASKED ME TO MOVE IN ,I CAME AROUND TO IT AND MOVED IN.

IT WAS ALL GOOD FOR A COUPLE OF MONTH'S.

WE DID EVERYTHING TOGETHER,SHE TAUGHT ME MANY THING'S IN LIFE.

LIKE HOW TO LOVE AND CARE ABOUT SOMEONE,AND HOW TO MAKE TRUE LOVE TO SOMEONE YOU CARE ABOUT.

I LOVE HER AND HER KIDS.

I GOT UP EVERY MORNING ,TOOK HER KIDS TO SCHOOL.

LIFE WAS GOOD FOR AWHILE,THEN THINGS TURNED AROUND.

PHONE CALLS STARTED COMING IN FROM MANY MEN'S,MEN'S EVEN KNOCKING AT THE DOOR.

I ASKED HER WHATS GOING ON,SHE EXPLAIN HOW SHE USE TO FOOL WITH MANY MEN IN THE PAST.

I LOST RESPECT FOR HER,FOR ONE REASON ,SHE SHOULD HAVE TOLD ME.

AN SHE SHOULD HAD TOLD THE MEN SHE HAD SOMEONE ,DON'T CALL ARE COME AGAIN.

SO WE STARTED HAVING PROBLEMS ,AND I PACKED UP MY STUFF AND LEFT.

ME AND MY EX KEPT IN TOUCH,AND EVENTALLY I DID THE WRONG THING,BY GOING BACK.

AFTER A COUPLE DAYS BACK WITH HER, I CATCH HER ARGUING ON THE PHONE WITH A MAN.

IASKED WHAT WAS GOING ON.

FOLDER: UNFILED

Notes: I FOUND OUT SHE WAS TALKING TO A EX,ABOUT SOME JEWELERY HE HAD OF HERS.

SHE SAID SHE WANTED IT BACK,BUT AT THE SAME TIME SHE SAID HE WAS CRAZY.

I ASKED WHY SHE DIDN'T TELL ME FIRST BEFORE SHE DID IT.

I TOLD HER WAS IT WORTH RISKING YOUR LIFE AND YOUR KIDS LIFE, FOR SOMETHING THAT COULD BE REPLACED.

BEFORE I KNEW IT ,A KNOCK AT THE DOOR.I LOOKED OUT THE WINDOW AND IT WAS HER EX WITH A GUN.

AM THINKING MY LIFE IS OVER,HE TRY'S TO BREAK IN THE HOUSE, I TOLD HER AND HER KIDS, TO GO HIDE.

I GOT A BASEBALL BAT AND WAITED, TO SEE IF HE WOULD BREAK IN.

HE DIDN'T KNOW I WAS THIER, SO MY FRIEND CALLED THE POLICE.

THE POLICE WAS TAKING TO LONG,SO I CALLED FAMILY TO TELL THEM TO COME HELP ME.

ABOUT TIME MY FAMILY ARRIVED,THE POLICE ARRIVED.THEY ARRESTED HIM AND MY FAMILY TALKED ME IN TO LIVING HER.

I SAID I WAS GOING TO SPEND ONE LAST NIGHT WITH HER.BECAUSE I KNOW SHE WAS SCARED.

SO IN THE MORNING I PACKED MY CLOTHES AND WENT HOME,LIFE WAS NOT TO GREAT FOR ME AT THIS TIME.

THEN ONE DAY A FRIEND SAID ,LETS GO JOB HUNTING AT THE CASINO'S.

I DIDN'T WANT TO WORK AT THE CASINO'S, BUT I WENT AND THE FUNNY PART IS ,THEY HIRED ME AND NOT MY FRIEND.

I EVENTALLY LANDED A JOB AT ONE OF THE LOCAL CASINO'S,SO I WAS PROUD OF MYSELF.
I MEET A SWEETHEART AT WORK,WE STARTED TALKING AND DATING.
BEFORE I KNEW IT,I WAS ENGAGED,ME AND MY FIANCEE HAD PROBLEMS.
SHE HAD BEEN THREW SO MUCH,SHE WAS TAKING IT OUT ON ME.
SO AFTER AWHILE,I WAS GETTING TIRED OF IT,EVEN THOUGH SHE HAD PROBLEMS,I STUCK WITH HER.
SHE GOT ME INTO CHURCH AND WAS DOING GOOD,HER FATHER WAS A PREACHER.
BUT THE PROLEMS WE HAD DESTROYED US,IT WASN'T JUST HER ,IT WAS ME TO.
SO BEFORE I KNEW IT ,I WAS TURNING BACK TO MY OLD SELF.

FROM: ANTHONY WILLIAMS (ANTHONY.WILLIAMS73@YAHOO.COM)

TO: ANTOHNY.WILLIAMS73@YAHOO.COM

DATE: SUNDAY, JUNE 15, 2008 1:52:33 PM

SUBJECT:

I STARTED SLEEPING AROUND AGAIN,EVEN WITH MY EX FIANCE COUSIN,I DIDN'T CARE AS LONG AS I WAS HAPPY.

I DATED MY EX COUSIN FOR AWHILE AND FELTED GUILTY,SO I TOLD MY EX ABOUT THE AFFAIR.

WHY DID I DO THAT,THEY ENDED UP IN A FIGHT,NOW AM FILLING DOWN BECAUSE I WAS THE CAUSE OF IT.

MY EX FATHER THE PREACHER,GOT MAD AND CURSE ME OUT,I WOULDN'T BELIEVE A PREACHER WOULD DO THAT.

ME AND MY EX,EVENTALLY BECAME FRIENDS ,AND STARTED FOOLING AROUND AGAIN,WHY ME I ASKED MYSELF WOULD I DO THIS AGAIN,JUST CRAZY AND FREAKY,I GUEST.

I REALIZED I SHOULDN'T BE FOOLING WITH MY EX,SO I LEFT HER ALONG.
SO I CONTINUE TO WORK AT ONE OF THE LOCAL CASINOS,FOR ABOUT 2 YEARS.

BEFORE I KNEW IT ,LADIES FROM EVERYWHERE STARTED HITTING ON ME.
I WAS WORKING ONE DAY AND THIS LADY ,APPROACH ME,SHE TOLD ME,SHE WAS FROM DALLAS TX.
SO WE EXCHANGED NUMBERS,WE TALKED ALL THE TIMES,EVERY OTHER WEEKENED SHE CAME TO SEE ME.
I STARTED FALLING FOR HER,THEN ONE DAY SHE ASKED ME TO MOVE TO DALLAS WITH HER.
I TOLD HER TO GIVE ME TIME AND I WOULD MOVE,SHE WANTED MEMOVE THAN ARE THATS WAS IT.
SO I WASN'T READY,SO WE BROKE UP,IT DIDN'T MATTER BECAUSE A NEW CO-WORKER STARTED HITTING ON ME.WE STARTED KICKING IT FOR AWHILE,AND ENDING UP SLEEPING WITH EACH OTHER.

FROM: ANTHONY WILLIAMS (ANTHONY.WILLIAMS73@YAHOO.COM)

TO: ANTOHNY.WILLIAMS73@YAHOO.COM

DATE: FRIDAY, JUNE 20, 2008 9:12:14 AM

SUBJECT:

I DIDN'T REALLY LIKE HER, EVEN THOUGH SHE WAS PRETTY AND FINE.
IO DIDN'T LIKE HER BECAUSE,MONEY ALWAYS COME OUT OF HER MOUTH.

AGAIN I MEET ANOTHER LADY,WHILE I WAS WORKING,WE STARTED DATING.

WE WERE DOING GOOD ,UNTIL ONE OF HER FRIENDS GOT MAD,BECAUSE MY GIRL LIKED HANGING OUT WITH ME,ALL THE TIMES.

SO SHE PLOTTED UP A PLAN TO BREAK UP US,SHE GOT A GIRL TO CALL MY FRIEND AND SAY WE WERE SLEEPING AROUND.

SO MY FRIEND ASKED ME WAS IT TRUE,I TOLD HER NO,SHE DIDN'T BELIEVE ME,SO I BROKE IT DOWN TO HER.

FROM: ANTHONY WILLIAMS (ANTHONY.WILLIAMS73@YAHOO.COM)

TO: ANTOHNY.WILLIAMS73@YAHOO.COM

DATE: FRIDAY, JUNE 20, 2008 12:34:30 PM

SUBJECT:

I TOLD HER ,HOW CAN I SLEEP WITH ANYONE,WHEN AM AT WORK ALL THE TIMES,ARE AM WITH HER ALL DAY.

I TOLD HER, WHEN SHE FINDS OUT HER FRIEND DID IT,DON'T CALL ME BACK.

BECAUSE IF YOU CANT TRUST ME,WE DON'T NEED TO BE TOGETHER.
LIKE I KNEW IT,SHE FOUND OUTH ER FRIEND WAS JEALOUS,BUT I WASN'T GOING BACK TO MY EX.

I STARTED FOCUSING ON MY WORK MORE,AND LESS ON LADIES.

I WAS DOING GOOD,I MADE EMPLOYEE OF THE MONTH ,TWO TIMES,MOVING UP IN THE COMPANY.

I TRANSERD TO ANOTHER DEPARTMENT, AT MY JOB,IT WAS GOOD AT FIRST,UNTIL ONE OF MY SUPERVISORS ,WAS HAVING A BAD DAY.

I JUST ASKED AFELLOW EMPLOYEE,TO SWITCH DUTIES WITH ME,BECAUSE IT WAS DONE REGULAR AT MY PLACE OF EMPLOYMENT.

MY SUPERVISOR DIDN'T LIKE IT,SO HE STARTED YELLING AT ME.

I TOLD HIM ,I WAS OT A CHILD AND WAS NOT GOING TO TALK TO ME CRAZY.

SO HE SAID WAIT TILL EVERYONE GO ,AND WE WILL DISCUSS THE PROLEM.

SO EVERYONE LEFT AND HE HAD ANOTHER PLAN,HE STARTED YELLING AT ME AGAIN, I TOLD HIM AGAIN NOT TO YELL.

SO HE CALMED DOWN AND I EXPLAIN WHY I WANTED TO TRADE DUTIES AT WORK.

HE GOT MAD AGAIN AND STARTED AGAIN ,TO YELL AT ME LIKE I WAS TEN YEARS OLD.

FROM: ANTHONY WILLIAMS (ANTHONY.WILLIAMS73@YAHOO.COM)

TO: ANTOHNY.WILLIAMS73@YAHOO.COM

DATE: SATURDAY, JUNE 21, 2008 1:04:15 PM

SUBJECT:

I THOUGHT I WAS DOING THE RIGHT THING,I TOLD HIM I WAS GOING TO HIS BOSS.

HE DIDN'T LIKE THAT,SO HE CALLED SECURITY ON ME WHILE I WAS LOOKING FOR HIS BOSS.

THE SECURITY GUARD CAME AND TOLD ME,HE CALLED,BUT HE KNEW MY BOSS WAS LYING BECAUSE HE SAID HE ALWAYS DO THAT.
SO THE SECURITY GUARD TOLD ME TO LEAVE,AND TELL HUMANRESOURCES THE NEXT DAY.

THE NEXT DAY I WENT TO HR,AND THEY ACTED LIKE THEY WERE SO CONCERN.THEY TOLD ME TO STAY OFF AND LET THEM INVESTIGATE.

SO I DIDN'T HEAR ANYTHING IN ACOUPLE OF DAYS,SO I CALLED THEM, THEY TOLD ME THEY WILL CALL.

FROM: ANTHONY WILLIAMS (ANTHONY.WILLIAMS73@YAHOO.COM)

TO: ANTOHNY.WILLIAMS73@YAHOO.COM

DATE: SATURDAY, JUNE 21, 2008 1:30:52 PM

SUBJECT:

ONE DAY ON A SATURDAY,THEY TOLD ME TO COME TO WORK AND TELL MY SIDE OF THE STORY.

I ARRIVED TO WORK TO GET A PINK SLIP,SAYING I CURSED HIM OUT,WHEN HE KNEW I DIDN'T.

THE FUNNY PART IS,MY COWORKERS AND SO CALL FRIENDS LIED AND SAID I DID.EARLY ON TAHT DAY MY FRIENDS SAID THEY WERE GOING TO BE ON MY SIDE.

I DIDN'T WORRY ABOUT IT,I TOLD THEM,I DIDN'T NEED A JOB WITH PEOPLE LIKE YOU.

I FOUND A JOB IN ABOUT 3 DAYS,AT ANOTHER CASINO,I WAS DOING GOOD AT MY NEW JOB.

THEN AGAIN LADIES STARTED HITTING ON ME AGAIN AND NOTICING ME .SO I EVENTUALLY STARTED DATING ONE OF MY COWORKERS.

FROM: ANTHONY WILLIAMS (ANTHONY.WILLIAMS73@YAHOO.COM)

TO: ANTOHNY.WILLIAMS73@YAHOO.COM

DATE: SATURDAY, JUNE 21, 2008 1:56:47 PM

SUBJECT:

SHE WAS PRETTY AND FINE,BUT HAD A FAMILY ,WHICH I WASN'T READY FOR.
SHE HAD FIVE KIDS AND I HAD NONE,SHE TOLD HER KIDS,SHE HATED THEM.
SO AM THINKING,WHAT WOULD MAKE ME WANT TO BES WITH A PERSON LIKE THAT.
SHE EVEN ASKED ME TO MARRY HER ,I WASN'T READY,SO WE BROKE UP.
THEN IT SEEM LIKE WOMEN FROM EVERYWHERE,WANTED TO SLEEP WITH ME.I ASKED MYSELF WHY ,I DON'T HAVE ANYTHING.
I WAS HAVING SEX WITH SUPERVISORS,SECURITY GUARDS,WHO EVER WANTED ME.
THEN THE WORST THING IN LIFE HAPPEN TO ME,MY MOTEHR HAD A STROKE AT THE HOUSE.IT WAS HARD TO SEE MY MOTHER SICK AND DOWN.

FROM: ANTHONY WILLIAMS (ANTHONY.WILLIAMS73@YAHOO.COM)

TO: ANTOHNY.WILLIAMS73@YAHOO.COM

DATE: SATURDAY, JUNE 21, 2008 2:10:43 PM

SUBJECT:

IT SCARRED ME BECAUSE I NEVER SEEN ANYONE HAVING A STROKE BEFORE.
MY DAD DIED OF CANCER WHEN I WAS YOUNGER,BUT WE WERE PREPARED
BECAUSE THE DOCTOR ALREADY INFORM US.
MY MOTHER WAS A FIGHTER,SHE SURVIVED IT AND CAME OUT THE
HOSPITAL THE SAME DAY.
UNFORTUNALY SHE HAD ANOTHER STROKE THE SAME DAY.
I WAS WORRIED ABOUT HER,SHE STAYED IN THE HOSPITAL FOR ABOUT A
MONTH.
I WAS THIER FOR HER EVERYDAY,ME AND MY FAMILY,I WOULDN'T LEAVE HER
SIDE ,UNTIL I KNEW SHE WAS BETTER.
SHE TOOK CARE OF ME WHEN I WAS SICK,NOW ITS MY TURN.

FROM: ANTHONY WILLIAMS (ANTHONY.WILLIAMS73@YAHOO.COM)

TO: ANTOHNY.WILLIAMS73@YAHOO.COM

DATE: SUNDAY, JUNE 22, 2008 1:14:59 PM

SUBJECT:

MY MOTHER GOT OUT OF THE HOSPITAL,SHE WASN'T PERFECT,BUT SHE WAS DOING ALRIGHT.

I WENT BACK TO WORK,WITH A DIFFERENT MIND SET,I WANTED TO BE MARRIED.

I WAS AT WORK ONE DAY,WHEN THIS GODDESS PASS BY,I FLIRTED WITH HER AND SHE LIKED IT.

WE EVENUALLY STARTED DATING,IT WAS GOING ,BUT I MESS UP THE RELATIONSHIP WITH HER.

I WAS SO DEDICATED TO HELPING MY MOM,i DIDN'T HAVE TIME TO DO ANYTHIG ELSE.

i DIDN'T WANT TO SPEND NIGHTS WITH MY GIRLFRIEND, BECAUSE I WAS SCARED SOMETHING WOULD HAPPEN TO MY MOTHER.

FROM: Anthony Williams (anthony.williams73@yahoo.com)

TO: antohny.williams73@yahoo.com

DATE: Sunday, June 22, 2008 1:25:08 PM

SUBJECT:

SO MY RELATIONSHIP ENED,I STARTED THINKING ABOUT WHAT MY MOM WOULD WANT ME TO DO.
I KNOW SHE WOULD WANT ME TO LIVE MY LIFE,EVEN THOUGH,AM NOT GOIG TO EVER STOP TAKING CARS OF HER.
I EVENTUALLY RAN TO THAT SPECIAL LADY,ONE DAY AT THE MALL.

SHE WORKED WITH ME,WE STARTED DATING AND IT WAS PERFECT,BUT I KNEW SOMETHING WOULD GO WRONG.

IT SEEMS LIKE WHEN EVER AM HAPPY,SOMETHING ALWAYS GO WRONG.
I FELL IN LOVE WITH HER,NOW THAT DARK CLOUD IS OVER MY HEAD.

MY GIRLFRIEND TOLD ME THAT HER KID DAD IS JEALOUS OF US, NOW THAT SHE HAD SOME ONE IN HER LIFE.

FROM: ANTHONY WILLIAMS (ANTHONY.WILLIAMS73@YAHOO.COM)

TO: ANTOHNY.WILLIAMS73@YAHOO.COM

DATE: MONDAY, JUNE 23, 2008 4:25:40 PM

SUBJECT:

HE LEFT HIS GIRLFRIEND TO START TROUBLE,BECAUSE HE DIDN'T WANT HER TO BE HAPPY.

SO THE DRAMA STARTS,HE STARTED COMING OVER HER HOUSE,STARTING TROUBLE.

I TALKED TO MY GIRL SISTER AND SHE TOLD ME ,HE HAD BEEN BEATING HER UP.

I GOT IN TOUCH WITH HIM AND ASKED HIM TO COME FIGHT ME,HE DIDN'T WANT ANY.

HE JUST LIKE BEATING ON LADIES,HE WASN'T A MAN,SO I CONVINCED HER TO MOVE IN WITH HER SISTER.

HE FOUND OUT WERE SHE STAY AND WENT OVER THIER,BROKE IN AND BEAT UP MY GIRL AND HER SISTER.

BUT LUCKY ENOUGH THE SISTER CALLED THE POLICE,MY GIRL HAD BEEN THREW SO MUCH PAIN AND DRAMA.
IT DROVE US CRAZY,SO SHE HAD TO GET HER MIND RIGHT,SO IT LEAD TO US BREAKING UP.
WE REMAIN FRIENDS,EVEN TO THIS DAY,I STILL HAVE LOVE FOR HER.

NOW AM FOCUS ON MY WORK,SINCE AM SINGLE AGAIN.
I FOUND OUT A NEW JOB WAS COMING TO TOWN,SO I PUT IN A
APPLICATION.

THEY CALLED ME AND HIRED ME,I WAS HAPPY,I WENT TO THIS JOB ,FOCUSE
ON DOING WHAT I HAD TO DO.

I WAS WORKING 12 HOURS A DAY,I DIDN'T HAVE TIME TO DO
ANYTHING,BUT SLEEP AND WORK.

THEN I MEET THIS SPECIAL LADY,BEFORE I KNEW IT ,WE WERE A COUPLE.

I STARTED THINKING TO MY SELF,THAT AM NOT RIGHT,EVERY GIRL I GET
WITH , I SAY AM IN LOVE WITH.

I KNOW I DIDN'T LOVE THESE WOMEN,ALTOUGH I THOUGHT I DID,I WAS
JUST A SEX ADDICT AND THAT WAS MY LOVE.

SO AFTER AWHILE ME AND PERSON HAD PROBLEMS AND WE BROKE UP.

THAT WAS FINE,BECAUSE I HAD A COWORKER WHO SAID ,HE WAS GOING TO INTRODUCE ME TO HIS COUSIN.

I THOUGHT SHE WAS GOING TO BE URGLY,BUT SHE WAS BEAUTIFUL AND NICE.

IT WAS LOVE AT FIRST SIGHT,WE HIT IT OFF, WE WERE PERFECT FOR EACH OTHER.

SHE WAS A GOOD WOMAN,SHE WAS LIKE ME,WORK AND BE AT HOME.

I ASKED HER TO MARRY ME AND SHE SAID YES,I TOLD EVERYONE BECAUSE THIS WAS MY FIRST TRUE LOVE,WE STARTED PLANNIG OUR WEDDING.

----- FORWARDED MESSAGE ----
FROM: ANTHONY WILLIAMS (ANTHONY.WILLIAMS73@YAHOO.COM)
TO: ANTOHNY.WILLIAMS73@YAHOO.COM
DATE: SATURDAY, JULY 12, 2008 12:25:03 PM
SUBJECT:

EVERY THING WAS FINE AT FIRST,THEN THE MOTHER DIDN'T LIKE THE IDEAL ,HER DAUGHTER WAS LEAVING THE NEST.

I WOULD CALL FOR MY FIANCE AND SHE WOULD CURSE ME OUT,FOR NO REASON. AFTER AWHILE I GOT TIRED OF IT,SO IT LEAD TO PROBLEMS.

I TOLD MY FIANCE ,LETS NOT GET MARRIED BECAUSE I DIDN'T WANT HER TO HAVE PROBLEMS WITH HER MOTHER.

SO WE CAME FRIENDS AND GREW FURTHER APART,SO IT KIND OF HURT ME,SO I STARTED SLEEPING AROUND AGAIN.

IT WAS MY THERAPY TO FORGET ABOUT HER,I KNEW IT WAS WRONG,BUT I DIDN'T CARE,SO I CONTINUE TO WORK JOB TO JOB.

FROM: ANTHONY WILLIAMS (ANTHONY.WILLIAMS73@YAHOO.COM)

TO: ANTOHNY.WILLIAMS73@YAHOO.COM

DATE: SUNDAY, JULY 13, 2008 12:05:27 PM

SUBJECT:

----- FORWARDED MESSAGE ----

FROM: ANTHONY WILLIAMS (ANTHONY.WILLIAMS73@YAHOO.COM)

TO: ANTOHNY.WILLIAMS73@YAHOO.COM

DATE: SUNDAY, JULY 13, 2008 12:05:08 PM

SUBJECT:

----- FORWARDED MESSAGE ----

FROM: ANTHONY WILLIAMS (ANTHONY.WILLIAMS73@YAHOO.COM)

TO: ANTOHNY.WILLIAMS73@YAHOO.COM

DATE: SATURDAY, JULY 12, 2008 12:41:39 PM

SUBJECT:

THATS WHEN I MEET A GIRL AT WORK,BUT I HAD NO INTENTIONS WITH HER,WE WERE FRIENDS FOR A YEAR.

I TOLD HER MY PROBLEMS AND SHE TOLD ME HERS,I HAD STOP HAVING SEX FOR ABOUT 7 MONTHS.

MY FREIND KNEW THIS,SHE USED THIS TO ADVANTAGE AND CALLED ME ONE DAY SAYING SHES COMING OVER.

SHE TOLD ME SHE WANTED ME,I THOUGHT SHE WAS PLAYING,BUT SHE CAME AND KNEW I HAD NOT DONE ANYTHING IN AWHILE.

SHE SEDUCED ME AND WHEN WE WERE THREW ,SAID AM PREGNANT,I SAID RIGHT ,I HADN'T HAD A CHILD IN ALL THESE YEARS I DIDN'T THINK I COULD MAKE ONE.

I ASKED HER TO TAKE A TEST,SHE SAID SHE WASN'T,SO I WENT ON WITH MY LIFE AND MY FRIEND DISAPEARED.I DID NOT HERE FROM HER ,UNTIL AYEAR LATER.

SHE CALLED AND SAID AM PREGNANT BY YOU AND JUST DIDN'T ,TELL ME.

I FOUND OUT MY KIDS MOTHER LIED TO ME ABOUT BEING PREGNANT,I DIDN'T BELIEVE THE CHILD WAS MINE.

THEN I HAD TO TELL MY NEW GIRL FRIEND ABOUT IT ,SHE WASN'T VERY HAPPY.

I TOOK A DNA TEST AND FOUND OUT I WAS THE FATHER,SO WE WENT TO COURT ,AND I PUT MYSELF ON CHILD SUPPORT.

ME AND MY KIDS MOTHER,DON'T REALLY GET ALONE,BUT I DON'T HATE HER.

NOW I HAVE TO WORK HARDER,TO MAKE SURE MY CHILD IS NOT HUNGRY. THE JOB AM AT NOW,DOESN'TPAY MUCH,AND THEY TALK CRAZY TO YOU.

I KNEW AWAY TO MAKE SOME MOEY,I STARTED SELLING DRUGS AGAIN.

THE FUNNY PART WAS,I WAS ONLY SELLING TO MY CO-WORKERS,THEY ALL HAD DRUG PROBLEMS.

AFTER AWHILE,I KNEW THIS WAS NOT FOR ME ,I HAD TO FIND ME A BETTER JOB.

I FOUND ME ANOTHER JOB AND STILL STRUGGLING,KNOE AM BACK TO MY OLD WAYS,SLEEPING AROUND.

ONE THING I REALIZED OVER ALL THESE YEARS ABOUT WOMEN,IS THE ONES I BEEN WITH,DON'T WANT NOTHING.

I LISTEN TO ALL OF THEM,TELL ME ABOUT HOW THIER MAN CHEATED AND HIT THEM.

HOW HE DIDN'T WANT TO DO ANYTHING WITH THEM,THEY WANT A MAN WHO GOING TO LOVE THEM.

THATS A LIE,BECAUSE I TREAT THEM ALL LIKE QUEENS,AND THEY STILL RAN BACK TO THE ONE WHO TREAT THEM LIKE DIRT.

AFTER A COUPLE OF YEARS AT MY JOB,I MEET MY WIFE,WE DATED FOR A COUPLE OF MONTHS,THEN DECIDED TO GET MARRIED.

IT WAS A MISTAKE,SHE WAS NOT READY,I SEEN THE SIGNS,BUT ENOUGH THEM.

NOW AM GOING TO GET A DIVORCE,SO I CAN BE WITH SOMEONE WHO WANTS TO MARRY ME AND LOVE ME.

I FOUND ME A BETTER JOB ANDAND TRYING TO MAKE MY LIFE BETTER,FOR ME.

SO WHAT AM TRYING TO SAY ,DON'T LET ANYONE TAKE YOUR DREAMS AWAY,I GOT A POEM THATS GOING TO BE PUBLISH AND A BOOK.

ALWAYS DO THE BEST YOU CAN IN LIFE,ANDSTAY AWAY FROM DRUGS.

YOUR FRIEND ANTHONY WILLIAMS

Printed in the United States
by Baker & Taylor Publisher Services